BEAUTIFUL AIRS & BALLADS OF THE BRITISH ISLES FOR CELLO

CRAIG DUNCAN

WWW.MELBAY.COM

Preface

This collection includes 30 traditional Irish, Scottish and English melodies that are beautifully suited to the cello. Traditional airs, love songs, songs of home and longing as well compositions by Turlough O'Carolan and J. Scott Skinner make up the content. Stylistic phrasing, variations and suggested chord changes aid in interpreting the tunes.

The titles are mostly in alphabetical order to keep the two-page arrangements on adjacent pages. "Loch Lomond" follows "Red is the Rose", as they are essentially the same melody and the arrangements could be played together. "Gentle Maiden" and "Give Me Your Hand" can be performed together in a nice medley.

I wish you great joy in performing these heartfelt melodies.

Craig Duncan

Contents

Call the Ewes

Ca' the Yowes tae the Knowes

Traditional Scottish
lyrics Robert Burns

Believe Me if All Those Endearing Young Charms

Traditional Irish Air
lyrics Thomas Moore 1808

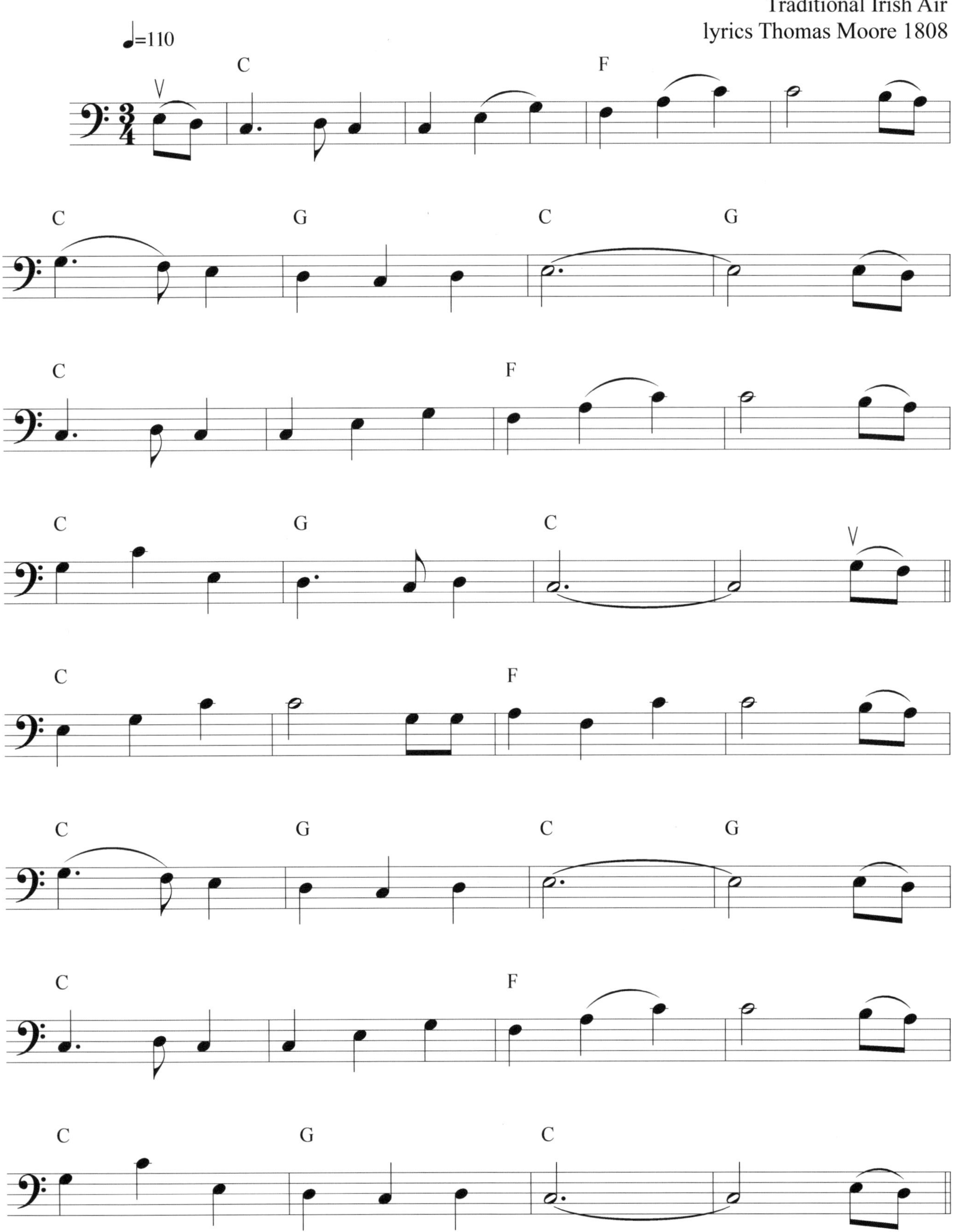

C F
C G C G
C F
C G C
C F
C G C G C
F C G
Am C F
C G C

Bonny at Morn

Traditional Northumberland Tune

Capo 3:

♩=76

Em Gm — *D* F

Em Gm — *D* F — *C* E♭

Em Gm — *D* F

Em Gm — *D* F — *C* E♭

Em Gm — *D* F — *Bm* Dm

C E♭ — *D* F — *Em* Gm

Em Gm — *D* F — *Bm* Dm

C E♭ — *D* F — *Em* Gm

Em
Gm
D
F
Em
Gm
D
F
C
E♭
Em
Gm
D
F
Em
Gm
D
F
C
E♭
Em
Gm
D
F
Bm
Dm
C
E♭
D
F
Em
Gm
Em
Gm
D
F
Bm
Dm
C
E♭
D
F
Em
Gm

Carolan's Concerto

Turlough O'Carolan

♩=80

G D G D G C D

G D G C G D G

C G Am D

G D G C G D G

G D G D C G D G

Am D C G Am D C

G Am D G Am

G D G D G 1. G 2.

ritard last time

Carolan's Draught

Turlough O'Carolan

The Clergy's Lamentation

Turlough O'Carolan

The Coulin

An Chúilfhionn / An Coolin

Traditional Irish

Danny Boy

Londonderry Air

Traditional Irish

Down by the Sally Gardens

The Maids of Mourne Shore

Traditional Irish

Fair Flower of Northumberland

Fanny Power

Turlough O'Carolan

Gentle Maiden

Traditional Irish

Give Me Your Hand

Hector the Hero

O wail for the mighty on battle; Loud lift ye the coronach strain;
For Hector the Hero, of deathless fame, will never come back again.

J. Scott Skinner/Scotland

John Anderson, My Jo

Traditional Scottish

♩=104

Dm C

Dm F Am

F C Gm C F C

Dm Dm C Dm 1, 3. 2.

Fine

Dm C B♭ Am A

Dm C B♭ A sus A

Gm C B♭ A Dm

Gm Dm C Dm

D.C. al Fine

Jock O' Hazeldean

Traditional Scottish

G D/F♯ Em G/D C
D G D/F♯ Em
G/D C D G C G
G D/F♯ Em G/D C
D G D/F♯ Em
G/D C D G C G
C G
D/F♯ Em C G D/F♯
Em G/D C D G
ritard

Niel Gow's Lament

Niel Gow's Lament for the Death of his Second Wife

Paddy's Green Shamrock Shore

Traditional Irish

Pretty Girl Milking Her Cow

Am G
Am G F
Am G
Am Em Am G
C G
C F G
Em Am G
Am Em Am
Am Em Am
ritard

The melody of this song is an Irish version of the Scottish tune, *Loch Lomond.*

Red is the Rose

Traditional Irish Song

Loch Lomond

The Bonnie Banks of Loch Lomond

Traditional Scottish Air

Scarborough Fair

Traditional English

Dm C Dm F
Dm F Dm
Dm F C Dm
C Dm
Dm C Dm F
Dm F Dm
Dm F C Dm
C Dm
D.C. al Fine

She Moved Through the Fair

Sheebeg Sheemore

Sí Beag, Sí Mhór, The Bonnie Cuckoo

Traditional Irish

♩=106

The Skye Boat Song

Over the Sea to Skye

Traditional Scottish Song

Em C G
G Em Am D
Em C G
Em Am
Em B+ Em
Em Am Em B+
Em D G D
Em C G G
D Em C G

The South Wind

An Ghaoth Aneas

Traditional Irish

Star of the County Down

Traditional Irish

♩=116

Em C G D

Em Bm Em

C G D Em Am

Em G D

Em Bm

Em C G D

Em Am Em 1. Em 2.

Am Em

ritard

The Water is Wide

Am7
D
Bm
C
G
C
Am7
D7
G
G
C
G
Em
Am7
D
Bm
C
G
C
Am7
D7
G
G7sus
C
Fmaj7
C
Am
Dm7
G
Em
F
C
F
Dm7
G7
C
Em
F
C
F
Dm7
G7
C
Fmaj7
C
Fmaj7
C

Wild Mountain Thyme

Will Ye Go, Lassie, Go

Traditional Scottish Folk Song

G
B♭
D
F
G
B♭
D
F
G
B♭
D
F
G
B♭
D
F
Bm
Dm
G
B♭
D
F
G
B♭
D
F
D
F
G
B♭
D
F
G
B♭
D
F
G
B♭
D
F
Bm
Dm
G
B♭
D
F
G
B♭
D
F
G
B♭
D
F
G
B♭
D
F
Bm
Dm
G
B♭
ritard
D
F
G
B♭
D
F

Will Ye No Come Back Again

Bonnie Charlie

Traditional Scottish Tune